WILDLIFE CONSERVATION AS DONE BY EXPERTS

Animal Book Age 10
Children's Animal Books

BABY PROFESSOR
EDUCATION KIDS

Speedy Publishing LLC

40 E. Main St. #1156

Newark, DE 19711

www.speedypublishing.com

Copyright 2017

In this book, we're going to talk about what governments and conservationists do to protect wildlife. So, let's get right to it!

WHAT IS WILDLIFE CONSERVATION?

Wildlife conservation is the process of making sure that Earth's plants and animals are protected from going extinct. The goal of conservationists around the world is to make sure that the beauty and diversity of life is preserved for future generations.

In order to make sure that species thrive, conservationists work to keep the habitats where these species live preserved. There are over 1,000 species worldwide that are classified as endangered, which means they are at risk of going extinct.

DANGER TO WILDLIFE

There are less natural habitat areas every year. Even where animal and plant habitats are still in existence, they're often much less ideal for animals and plants than the lands and environments that were available to them in centuries past. There are many reasons why these important habitats are in decline. These are some of the main threats that habitats are subjected to:

CLIMATE CHANGE

The effects of global warming are causing the weather to change worldwide. Hot spells are much longer and the soil becomes parched. Storms are heavier causing flooding over vast areas. These extremes in climate can be seen around the world. When the climate shifts, the landscape changes as a result, and then animal and plant habitats are greatly affected.

Effects of Climate Change

White Rhino

OVERHUNTING AND POACHING

Although there are laws set in place to ensure that overhunting and poaching are stopped, they're not always enforced. It's true that we need many different types of animals for food, but many hunters are just killing for sport or trophies. Examples of animals that are hunted in this way are great white sharks, black rhinoceroses, African elephants, and cheetahs.

POLLUTION

Pesticides and other industrial toxins that are waste products of manufacturing are polluting our waterways. The majestic bald eagle nearly went extinct from DDT, which is a pesticide. After it became illegal to use DDT, the populations of bald eagles gradually increased and in 2007 the species was removed from the list of endangered species.

Illegal Logging

OVERUSE OF ANIMALS AND PLANTS FOR PRODUCTS

We'll continue to need animals and plants for food, for medicines, to create clothing, for sports, and many other reasons. The problem becomes when we overuse with no consideration for how removing individual animals and plants impacts their populations

If we take too many animals or plants from a specific species, eventually they won't be able to reproduce fast enough and their populations begin to decline.

DEFORESTATION

As humans increase in population, they clear land for houses and to plant crops. This leveling of forests causes a huge decrease in natural habitats. As populations of animals try to find new homes and new food sources, their numbers decrease. Sometimes the available habitats become so small that the animals die out.

Deforestation

INCREASING HUMAN POPULATION

The ever increasing population of humans is the major cause of almost all threats to wildlife. We're taken over land that used to be their domain.

We're killing animals and plants for food and other products such as medicines and clothing. We're even taking wild animals out of their natural habitats to keep them as pets, sometimes with disastrous consequences.

Sadly, many people and some governments are not concerned about the threat to endangered species. This, in many ways, is the biggest challenge to the work of conservationists. Educating people about wildlife conservation is very important.

Chobe National Park

PROTECTING ANIMALS AND THEIR HABITATS IN NATIONAL PARKS

One of the most important ways to conserve wildlife is to ensure that their habitats are not destroyed. This requires government involvement since the government's approval is required to establish national parks. Inside national parks, activities that harm wildlife, such as hunting or fishing, are not allowed.

In the United States, the first such park was Yellowstone. In 1872, it was established as a wildlife preserve and national park. From this beginning, the United States has converted vast areas of land to a total of 58 national parks.

Yellowstone National Park

A lion in Hwange National Park

Over 100 countries worldwide have done the same and there are now over 1,000 protected parks around the globe. All in all, about 2 million square miles has been set aside for preservation. Although this is a large area, compared to all the land on Earth it's about 3%.

CAPTIVE BREEDING

Captive breeding simply means that animals are encouraged to mate and produce offspring in zoos and preserves. Sometimes, the only animals of a particular species that still exist are the ones who live in these protected habitats.

With a systematic program that supports the animals, it's possible for their populations to increase to the point where they can once again be released into the wild.

Snow Leopards

African Oryx

A great example of how captive breeding can be successful is the reintroduction of the African oryx. In the 1970s, this long-horned antelope was overhunted to the brink of extinction. Tribesmen from Lake Turkana hunted the animals for their hides and their meat. In many native African cultures, their horns were considered to be magical charms.

In addition to this problem of being overhunted, the human population was crowding out the areas where oryxes lived. The last few animals were protected by zoos because the oryxes were extinct in the wild.

Through captive breeding, the number of oryxes began to increase and they were brought back to the wild in 2011. It will take time for them to move off the "vulnerable" list, but they have a chance to survive due to captive breeding.

Przewalski Horse

Another example of successful captive breeding is the reintroduction of the Przewalski horse. This wild horse was at one time extinct in the wild. Captive breeding has brought this species back. They are still endangered but their populations are beginning to increase.

KEEPING TRACK OF ANIMAL POPULATIONS

In order to protect animal populations in specific habitats, scientists need to know approximately how many of a particular species live in a designated area. There are three different ways that they track populations:

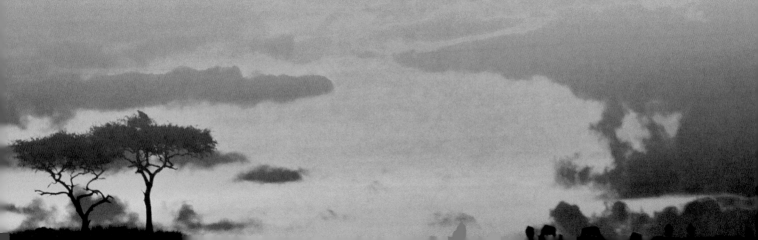

Cheetah

Buffalo

PHYSICAL EVIDENCE

Animals leave evidence of where they live. They drop feces on the ground. They leave tracks. They construct dens and burrows and leave leftover food at the places where they feed.

By going out into the field, scientists can observe this evidence and project the numbers of a specific population. Of course, this is a very scary method if you're tracking lions or pythons.

TRANSMITTERS

Tracking isn't only to figure out the size of populations. Some tracking is used to determine the migration paths of a particular species. New technology has created very small transmitters that scientists can use to keep track of animals.

White Tailed Deer

Wolf

These can be safely swallowed by the animal or placed under its skin. Some of these small devices allow scientists to pinpoint an animal's exact location using Global Positioning System technology, which is called GPS for short. Once they find several animals, they can track the migratory path of the population.

REMOTE CONTROL CAMERAS

Cameras operated by remote control are another way to keep track of animals. The cameras are protected in weatherproof cases. They are left outdoors near trails or areas where animals feed. When the animal passes by, a sensor is triggered and a photo is taken.

Sea Turtle

Tracking animals

PASSING LAWS TO PROTECT ANIMALS

Many countries have laws that protect endangered animals. People who break these laws are prosecuted and must serve time in jail or pay expensive fines. Unfortunately, not all countries have enacted or enforced these laws.

A lso, there are always people who break the law to hunt or poach. Poachers kill animals to get their horns, tusks, or fur. For example, elephants are killed to get their ivory since a kilogram is valued at $1000 or more.

Three of the most important conservation laws are:

THE ENDANGERED SPECIES ACT

Passed in the 1970s under President Richard Nixon, this law's goal is to prevent the extinction of endangered species.

Elephants

Tiger

THE CONVENTION ON INTERNATIONAL TRADE IN ENDANGERED SPECIES

This agreement was designed to protect endangered animals and plants from being exported and imported in products and as specimens from country to country.

THE RHINOCEROS AND TIGER CONSERVATION ACT

This act was specifically designed to protect species of rhinoceros and tigers, which are all on the endangered list.

BECOMING A WILDLIFE CONSERVATIONIST

If you love the outdoors and care about protecting plants and animals, you may want to think about becoming a wildlife conservationist in the future. You'll need to start by studying science and math in school. When you go to college, you can major in wildlife biology, agricultural science, or environmental science.

Most people working in this field have master's degrees.

Manatee

A typical day might include working outdoors to protect habitats from fire or dangerous insects. You might be checking soil samples to make sure they are not polluted or doing some research about species in a certain section of land.

Scientists believe that we're losing between 200-2,000 species to permanent extinction every year. By becoming a wildlife conservationist, you can help ensure that your children and grandchildren will be able to benefit from a world filled with biodiversity.

Migratory Birds

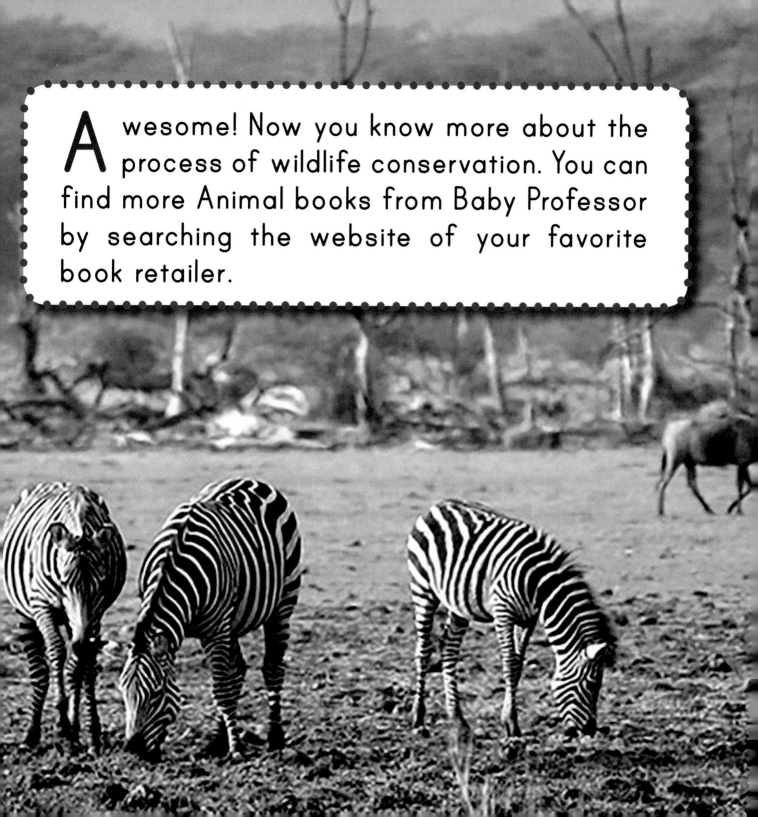

Awesome! Now you know more about the process of wildlife conservation. You can find more Animal books from Baby Professor by searching the website of your favorite book retailer.

Made in the USA
Coppell, TX
07 October 2020

39469985R00040